D1299430

HAUNTED BATTLEFIELDS

ANTIETAM

HISTORY AND LEGEND

BY

RUSSELL ROBERTS

PURPLE TOAD
PUBLISHING

HAUNTED

BATTLEFIELDS

ANTIETAM by Russell Roberts
GETTYSBURG by Russell Roberts
LITTLE BIGHORN by Earle Rice Jr.
VERDUN by Earle Rice Jr.

PUBLISHER'S NOTE
The data in this book has been researched in depth, and to the best of our knowledge is factual. Although every measure is taken to give an accurate account, Purple Toad Publishing makes no warranty of the accuracy of the information and is not liable for damages caused by inaccuracies.

ABOUT THE AUTHOR:
Russell Roberts has researched, written, and published numerous books for both children and adults. Among his books for adults are *Down the Jersey Shore, Historical Photos of New Jersey*, and *Ten Days to A Sharper Memory*. He has written over 50 nonfiction books for children. Roberts often speaks on the subjects of his books before various groups and organizations. He lives in New Jersey.

Printing   1   2   3   4   5   6   7   8   9

Publisher's Cataloging-in-Publication Data
Roberts, Russell.
    Antietam / Russell Roberts.
        p. cm.
Includes bibliographic references.
ISBN 9781624691140
1. Antietam, Battle of, Md., 1862--Juvenile literature. 2. United States--History--Civil War, 1861-1865--Fiction. 3. United States. President (1861-1865 : Lincoln). Emancipation Proclamation--Juvenile literature. 4. Antietam National Battlefield (Md.)—History. I. Series: Haunted Battlefields.
 E474.65 2015
 973.7336

Library of Congress Control Number: 2014945179

ebook ISBN: 9781624691157

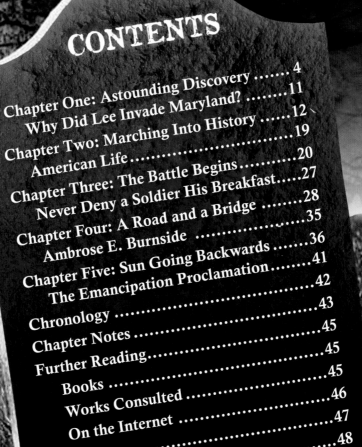

CONTENTS

CHAPTER

ONE

ASTOUNDING DISCOVERY

All the men are apparently jolly.[1]
—Private John W. Stevens, Confederate Army

Corporal Barton W. Mitchell was tired.

He was a member of the 27th Indiana, which was part of the Union's Army of the Potomac. It was September 13, 1862, and the army had been pursuing Robert E. Lee and his Confederate Army of Northern Virginia, which had invaded Maryland. The Union Army was currently outside the town of Frederick, Maryland, and marching to catch Lee. The march, in long columns along dirt roads under a still-warm September sun, had kicked up great clouds of swirling dust that choked officers and horses alike. So when Mitchell saw an opportunity to take a brief rest, he took it.

He flopped down in the shade of a large tree along a fence, enjoying the feel of the cool grass. He thought about the welcome the army had received in Frederick. People had poured out of their houses to greet the soldiers, waving American flags, cheering and yelling. Ladies had rushed out with buckets of water to offer the

★ ★ ★ ★ ★ ★ ★ ★ ★ ★ ★ ★ ★ ★ ★ ★ ★

Civil War soldiers on the march grabbed any opportunity they could for a rest. When Union soldier Barton W. Mitchell did so, he made a discovery of tremendous importance.

The federal army, and particularly General McClellan, was greeted enthusiastically when it marched through Maryland.

thirsty soldiers drinks as they passed. Some people had even rushed up to the Union commander, General George McClellan, and hugged his horse!

As Mitchell was lying on the ground, he noticed a bulky envelope in the grass nearby. Curious, he picked it up, and by doing so changed the course of the Civil War.

When he first looked inside the envelope, Mitchell felt a bolt of excitement. Inside was a piece of paper wrapped around three cigars. Then he noticed something odd about the paper the cigars were wrapped in. It wasn't a piece of scrap paper, or newspaper. It looked official. As he read it, Mitchell knew that he had made an amazing discovery.

The heading on the paper read, "Headquarters, Army of Northern Virginia, Special Orders, No. 191."[2] Mitchell knew this meant that the paper came from the

headquarters of General Robert E. Lee, head of the Confederate Army. It was dated September 9—just four days earlier—and contained orders from General Lee to his commanders. Lee was splitting his army up—a dangerous maneuver, but even more so because the rebels were in enemy territory.

This was secret information of the most special kind. It was as if Mitchell had been standing next to Lee and listening to him as he gave his orders. The Union Army now had information that they could use to destroy the Confederates!

Before the secret orders wound up in General McClellan's hands, McClellan had been uncertain of what the rebel commander was up to and was unwilling to stumble into a trap. When McClellan read Lee's orders, he got excited.

"Now I know what to do!" he exclaimed. He waved the paper in the air. "Here is a paper with which if I cannot whip 'Bobbie Lee' [Robert E. Lee] I will be willing to go home."[3]

So McClellan put his troops on a march to intercept Lee. Little did he know that by doing so he had embarked on the Battle of Antietam, one of the biggest battles of the Civil War. Days later, by the time the last wisps of cannon smoke had drifted away from the battlefield, some 23,100 men from both the Union and Confederate armies would be killed, wounded, or missing. It would be the single bloodiest day of the war.

And, as some Baltimore schoolboys found out over 100 years later, it was a day that some may still be repeating. . . .

***

Many school groups go to Antietam, which is a National Historic site. They come to study the battlefield, walk across the ground where many died, and drink in the unique atmosphere that cannot be explained in history books.

One of these areas is a place now called Bloody Lane. At the time of the battle it was just known as the Sunken Road—a long trench, several feet below ground level, that had been worn from the weight of farmers' wagons hauling grain to a nearby mill over the years.

During the battle, the Sunken Road was the site of tremendous fighting. Southern troops initially occupied the road. Union soldiers repeatedly attacked the rebel troops in the road, trying to force them out. The rebels held out fiercely. Dead and wounded men piled up all around and inside it.

Religious services were an important part of a soldier's life.

One of the Union brigades that continually attacked the rebels that day was the 69th New York, known as the "Irish Brigade." Composed largely of Irishmen, the soldiers charged into battle shouting their peculiar war cry in Gaelic (an ancient Irish language): *"Faugh a Ballagh"*, which means "Clear the Way" and sounds like the Christmas carol "Deck the Halls"—"Fa-a-bah-lah." The brigade lost 60 percent of their men as they charged the rebels over and over again, racing toward them through a blizzard of gunfire, all the while chanting their war cry.[4]

The Baltimore schoolboys wandered around the battlefield. They ended their day by meeting at the Sunken Road. Their teacher told them to write essays on what stood out most during their visit.

A few days later, as the teacher graded the essays, he noticed that many of the boys mentioned hearing "[Christmas] caroling in a foreign language" as they were waiting at Bloody Lane. He questioned the students in class, and found that many had heard what they described as voices repeating the chorus to "Deck the Halls" over and over again. The teacher asked the boys to sing what they had heard, and each repeated the sounds the same way: "Fa-la-la-lah."

The small map illustrates the location of the Antietam battlefield today. The larger one shows the position of the Union (in blue) and Confederate (in red) soldiers during the fighting.

CHAPTER ONE

Today the Sunken Road on the Antietam Battlefield is green and peaceful, but on the day of the battle it was filled with the bodies of Union and Confederate soldiers.

The teacher was stunned. He was an Antietam expert, and knew that the boys were repeating almost exactly the Gaelic war cry of the Irish Brigade—a sound that had not been heard in that place for over 100 years.

How could the boys know that sound—unless the Irish Brigade themselves were somehow, some way, still fighting at the Sunken Road, all the while chanting their special war cry?

Maybe for some, the Battle of Antietam is not yet over.

Lee's Army of Northern Virginia invaded Maryland in September 1862 for several reasons. That summer had been a good one for the Confederacy. They had defeated the Union in several battles. They had momentum. Lee felt that it was best to try to deliver a knockout punch to the North now.

It was also believed that a Maryland invasion would cause the so-called "Border State" to finally join the Confederacy and thus provide the rebel army with more fighting men.

Lee also hoped that by invading the Union, Northern citizens would turn against the war and elect Congressmen in the upcoming elections that favored negotiating an end to the war.

Finally, if the Confederates could defeat the Union again, it might convince Great Britain and France to recognize the Confederacy as a legitimate nation, winning support from those countries. The invasion culminated with the Battle of Antietam (which the Confederacy called the Battle of Sharpsburg).

General Robert E. Lee, leader of the Confederate Army, was a daring and resourceful commander who repeatedly beat larger Union armies.

CHAPTER

TWO

MARCHING INTO HISTORY

An old man was seen to pull off his shoes and give them to one of our barefooted soldiers, and ride off in his socks.[1]
—J.J. McDaniel, Confederate Army

To begin the invasion, Lee brought his army from Virginia across the Potomac River and into Maryland on September 4, 1862. The Southern soldiers agreed with Lee's reasoning for the invasion.

"If we ever expect to end [this war]," wrote a soldier from North Carolina, "we must invade the enemies country & make him feel the evils he is inflicting on us."[2]

The Confederate Army was in high spirits, confident and happy. One man wrote that there were "few moments . . . of excitement more intense"[3] than when they heard the song "Maryland, My Maryland" (which sounds similar to the holiday song "O Christmas Tree") being played by their bands as they marched.

As the rebel soldiers marched along, however, they did not impress the Marylanders they passed. Their uniforms were in rags, their bodies dirty, and their faces unshaven. Many of the soldiers were barefoot. It was said that they could be smelled before they

★ ★ ★ ★ ★ ★ ★ ★ ★ ★ ★ ★ ★ ★ ★ ★ ★ ★

When the Confederate Army crossed the river into Maryland, they hoped to find food that the picked-clean farms of northern Virginia could no longer provide.

could be seen. "They were the dirtiest men I ever saw," said one young man as the rebels passed.[4]

Within a few days, Lee admitted to Confederate President Jefferson Davis that the support he had hoped his invasion would cause in the Maryland people was not going to happen. One estimate is that only around 200 men became southern soldiers.[5] The Confederate army's poor appearance might have been a reason why Maryland men did not flock to join their ranks. "They looked on us in self-evident pity," said one Confederate officer.[6]

Still, the men were certain that when battle came, they would score a great victory. And why not? Despite being outnumbered and under-equipped, they had beaten the North repeatedly, most recently at Second Bull Run (also known as Second Manassas). They had all the confidence in the world in their generals.

At the Second Battle of Bull Run, Lee and the Confederates once again defeated the Union Army.

After the battles were over, the sad task of collecting bodies and wounded men begging for help took place.

The same could not be said for the men on the opposite side, in the Army of the Potomac. They had been soundly beaten time and again, and they blamed the incompetence of their leaders, especially the generals. Washington Roebling, who would someday build the Brooklyn Bridge, wrote that the Union soldiers "fight without an aim and without enthusiasm; they have no confidence in their leaders."[7]

President Abraham Lincoln was in a bind. He didn't want to turn to George McClellan again to reorganize the Union Army, but Lincoln had no one else he could call upon. After its defeat at Second Manassas the Union Army was a mess and its soldiers unhappy. The soldiers liked McClellan, and McClellan was organized. He was just poor at fighting.

In addition, after all the recent Confederate victories, Great Britain was considering recognizing the Confederacy as an independent country. If it did, and began helping the South by sending them money or supplies, the Union would likely never win the war. So Lincoln was desperate for someone to stop Lee. In his desperation, the president reluctantly put McClellan back in charge of the Union Army. As word spread to the troops that "Little Mac" was in command once again, their depression lifted and their confidence returned.

McClellan quickly reorganized the Union Army, and by September 7 they were moving to intercept Lee's troops. As they marched through Maryland, the Union troops received an enthusiastic welcome from its people, and it helped to raise their spirits even further.

"Flags floated from nearly every window and ladies waved their handkerchiefs from every balcony," wrote one soldier as he described the greeting the army received in Maryland.[8]

Then came the incredible stroke of good luck on September 13, when Lee's Special Orders 191 were found wrapped around some cigars. Suddenly, everything seemed to be going the Union's way.

On September 15, the Union Army arrived at the village of Sharpsburg and found the Confederates waiting for them just outside of town. McClellan selected the large, two-story brick farmhouse of Philip Pry as his headquarters.

Little did he know that by doing so, he was condemning the house to a place among the spirits, where the dead may still walk. . . .

***

Today, the Pry House on the Antietam Battlefield is a medical museum. It has only recently opened to the public. Before that, for many years it was closed and used for storage.

Two Union generals, wounded during the Battle of Antietam, were brought to this big brick house. One of them was Joseph Hooker. His injury was not serious and he soon recovered.

The other was named Israel B. Richardson. He was a popular figure among his men, who affectionately called him "Fighting Dick." While trying to organize an attack on the Sunken Road, Richardson was wounded by a shell fragment. He was carried to the Pry House, where his wound was examined and not considered serious.

However, this was a time before antibiotics were known, so even a scratch could become deadly. An infection set in to Richardson's wound. His wife, Fannie, came to Pry House to take care of him, but the infection gradually spread. Richardson died at Pry House on November 3, 1862, six weeks after the battle, his grieving wife by his side.

It seems that her grief became something more powerful than death itself.

One day over a century later, when the Pry House was still closed to the public, the wife of one of the Antietam park rangers happened to be at Pry House and saw a woman in old-fashioned clothing coming down the stairs. Impressed by the

According to some, the Pry House on the Antietam battlefield has been the scene of supernatural activity.

A ghostly figure has been seen on these stairs in the Pry House.

woman's attention to detail with her clothing, the wife asked her husband who the historical reenactor was.

The ranger stared at his wife. There was no such person at the park.

Sometime later, there was a fire in the Pry House. The fire severely damaged the second floor, which collapsed. As firefighters continued to battle the blaze, they looked at the house and saw an incredible sight.

There, in a second floor window, was a woman looking out at them. The only trouble was that the second floor had collapsed some time before. So the woman would have had to be floating in order to be seen from the window. After the fire was out, the house was searched top to bottom, but no woman was ever found.

A construction crew was hired to renovate the Pry House. However, the crew soon quit because the mysterious figure of a woman kept being seen inside the house. However, when the workers investigated, no woman was ever found.

Could all of these sightings have been the ghost of the distraught Fannie Richardson, her immense sadness keeping her eternally trapped at the House?

Even though it is now open to the public, the Pry House is still not at peace. Footsteps have been heard on the stairs, but no person is ever seen. Maybe the ghost of Fannie Richardson is still climbing up and down the stairs, vainly hoping that death won't take her husband.

What was life like in America in September 1862?

The typical middle-class family lived in row homes, small stand-alone wood frame houses, or even in apartments (known then as "French Flats"). Extended families were far more common, and aunts, uncles, grandparents, and single nieces and nephews all tended to live together. Young, single people usually did not live far away, but either in the house of their birth or in rooms nearby.

People usually bathed just once a week, often on Saturday night, so they'd be clean for Sunday church services. Indoor plumbing was not common, and whether one had toilet facilities depended on the local water and sewage system. Lots of people still used outhouses and indoor chamber pots, which had to be emptied. Toilet paper was unknown; leaves and old newspapers were used in its place.

Since there were no supermarkets, many people had gardens and fruit trees for growing food. Tomatoes, sweet corn, lettuce, cabbage and beans were items typically grown in vegetable gardens. Without refrigeration, food was either eaten fresh or preserved through means like pickling, smoking, or drying.

One of the most important items of clothing for men was a hat. Women never went anywhere without their parasols, which they used to shield their skin from the sun. It was believed that the lighter a woman's skin was, the better.

Typical clothing of the time of the Civil War

CHAPTER

THREE

THE BATTLE BEGINS

They stood and shot each other till the lines melted away like wax.[1]
—Isaac Hall, Union Army

Why did the Federal Army choose to set up near the town of Sharpsburg and Antietam Creek?

There are several answers to this question. The first is the infamous Special Orders 191—the one that Union Corporal Barton Mitchell found wrapped around those three cigars.

The order called for the Confederate Army to split up. The largest group was sent to Harpers Ferry, Virginia, to capture the 12,000 Union troops that occupied the town. Lee needed to establish a supply line (a route over which food, ammunition, and other items could be brought to his soldiers) and Harpers Ferry stood right in the way.

Military strategy dictates that you should never divide your army in the face of an enemy, particularly if your army is smaller

Union soldiers kept trying to cross Antietam Creek via this narrow stone bridge, and the Confederates kept shooting them down.

than theirs. Lee had about 50,000 men; McClellan had 70,000.[2] It was a risky and dangerous move for Lee to make.

However, he was a gambler. It was how he had won so many victories over a numerically superior foe, by doing the unexpected and taking risks. So why stop now?

But, if the enemy was to get wind of the division—as McClellan did by finding Special Orders 191—then the whole thing could blow up in Lee's face. All McClellan had to do was attack the divided pieces of the Confederate Army before they could reunite.

However, this was George McClellan—as cautious a general as ever lived. He was always convinced that he was outnumbered, even though he almost never was. So even with the great advantage of Special Orders 191, he moved slowly to find the Confederates. Meanwhile, a Confederate sympathizer (someone who favored the Confederacy) had witnessed McClellan receiving Special Orders 191. He rode to the Confederates and told them. This information quickly got back to Lee, who realized that McClellan knew his plans.

Lee ordered his army to reassemble at Sharpsburg, Maryland, a village where many of the local roads converged. Named after former Maryland governor Horatio Sharpe, it was a town of 1,300 people, some of whom worked at a nearby ironworks and most of whom worked on farms.[3]

Lee selected his positions carefully—the hills behind Antietam Creek. It was there that McClellan found the rebels, and that's why he put his troops into line of battle there beginning on September 15.

Still, he did not attack that day, nor the next. He wanted to be careful, after all. And as those days slipped away, so did more chances to attack the rebels before they had a chance to concentrate their army.

The attack began on the 17th at dawn, with the air still heavy and wet with morning mist. The initial Union assault struck near a small church of a religious group known as the Dunkards (or Dunker). Ironically, the Dunkards were pacifists (against war and violence).

The rebels were waiting nearby in the thirty-acre cornfield of farmer David R. Miller. As the guns roared, signaling the start of the battle, the door of a nearby farmhouse suddenly burst open and several terrified women came running out

Near the tiny Dunkard Church, one of the bloodiest battles of the Civil War began on the morning of September 17, 1862.

"like a flock of birds . . . hair streaming in the wind and children of all ages stretched out behind."[4] The firing from both sides suddenly ceased as a Confederate officer rode up and led them to safety.

When it resumed, the fire between the two sides became so intense that the cornstalks—in what would forever be known as "The Cornfield"—were cut down as if by a sharp knife. The soldiers were not much luckier.

"Men, I cannot say fell . . . ," wrote Major Rufus Dawes, "they were knocked out of ranks by the dozen."[5]   Still, the soldiers raced forward, ignoring as best they could the whizzing of deadly metal in the air all around them and getting swept up in the heat of battle. "The men are loading and firing with demoniacal fury and shouting and laughing hysterically," said Dawes of the fighting.[6]

The fighting there lasted five hours, with both sides repeatedly attacking and counterattacking.

General Joseph Hooker had formerly been in command of the entire Union Army of the Potomac, but after his defeat at Chancellorsville by the Confederates he was replaced as Lincoln desperately sought a general who could match Lee.

Eventually the fighting died down, as much as from the soldiers' exhaustion as from anything else. By this time, the wounded General Hooker had been brought to the Pry House, where the Union High Command were sitting on the front lawn in easy chairs brought out from the house's parlor.

It was around noon that the action switched to the center—and what would become known as Bloody Lane.

***

Over a century later, the cries and groans of the dying have long faded from Bloody Lane . . .

Or have they?

While the story of the Baltimore schoolboys hearing the ghostly cries of the Irish Brigade is perhaps the most famous story associated with Bloody Lane, there have been so many others that the sunken dirt road is considered the most haunted place on the battlefield.

People who go there to wander among the now-peaceful grass and trees often report that if you listen closely, you can still hear the screams of dying men, and the faint echo of guns firing. Some say they smell gun smoke. Others claim to see figures out of the corner of their eyes—faint, blurry images of men running,

Today Bloody Lane on the Antietam battlefield is peaceful and quiet —or is it?

CHAPTER THREE

Immediately after the battle was over, burial details came to Bloody Lane to collect the many bodies lying there. Is all this death the cause of supernatural activity there?

yelling, firing, and dying as they pitch face-first to the ground. But when they swing around to where they thought they saw the figures, there is nothing there.

Some people today lie on the soil of Bloody Lane. These folks report hearing cries, groans of pain, and men calling to each other. The sounds are whispered, but urgent. Sometimes there's a touch on the arm or a faint brush of the face, and the people leap up, wondering who did it.

But there's never anybody there.

Some believe that sudden, violent death is one of the causes of ghosts and spiritual activity. No one knows for sure.

One thing is certain, however. No one goes to Bloody Lane at night or lingers there when the sun starts to go down.

There was lots of hard fighting at Antietam this day. Most of the men did it because they believed it was their duty.

However, for some soldiers, there was another reason that they fought so hard, and it had to do with their breakfast.

The men under rebel commander John Bell Hood were tough fighters. Many had seen battle at Antietam the previous evening, when rebel and Union soldiers had tangled in preliminary fighting.

Since Hood's men had fought the night before, they were sent to the rear that morning to relax and get something to eat. Supplying soldiers with food was a constant problem in the Confederate Army, and the food that was issued now was the first they had seen in three days. Unfortunately, it was only flour. The men used it to make what were called "hoecakes," which could be cooked over a campfire.

Hood's men were just cooking their hoecakes when they received an urgent summons: Union troops were pushing the Confederates back. These soldiers had to go back to the front immediately and try to stop them.

The Confederate soldiers were furious. Here they were, just about to eat, and now they had to go fight. Again. "Just as we began to cook . . . we were ordered into formation," wrote a Georgia soldier. "I have never seen a more disgusted bunch of boys and mad as hornets."[7]

The angry Southerners attacked with a fury that smashed the Union soldiers and forced them to retreat. See what happens when you deny a soldier his breakfast?

General Hood

CHAPTER

FOUR

A ROAD AND A BRIDGE

*The soldier who is shot looks around for help with an imploring
agony of death on his face.*[1]
—*Rufus R. Dawes, Union Army*

As the fighting was slackening in the Cornfield, it was increasing in
and near the Sunken Road. Initially, the road was held by Confederate
troops. The road was a superior defensive position because it was
below the surface, and the soldiers in it could shoot without
exposing most of their bodies to enemy fire.

To make matters worse, many of the attacking Union troops had
just joined the army. They panicked when the bullets started flying
around them. "Troops didn't know what they were expected to do,
and sometimes, in the excitement, fired at their own men," said one
Connecticut soldier.[2]

Just to add to the Union soldiers' misery, a Confederate shot
burst into a row of nearby beehives. Swarms of angry, buzzing bees
poured out, furious that their homes had been destroyed, and
swarmed all around a group of Union troops.

Civil War battles often resulted in many casualties on both sides, partially because the two armies fought at such close quarters that men could not help getting killed or wounded.

As one historian described it, the Sunken Road became like a "great whirlpool, sucking more thousands into its vortex."[3] A carpet of dead and wounded Union soldiers lay before it. In it, another carpet, this time of dead and wounded Confederate soldiers, lay on the blood-soaked dirt. Shrieking horses, booming cannon, firing muskets, and screaming men created a thunderous sound that enveloped the entire area.

Finally, after several hours, the superior numbers and the greater fire power of the Union Army artillery prevailed, and the North cleared the Sunken Road of the remaining Confederate soldiers. Southern troops retreated in confusion and panic. Their withdrawal created a huge gap in Lee's line; this was McClellan's golden opportunity. If he sent Union troops flooding into this opening, he might have destroyed the entire Confederate Army. The Civil War might have ended right there.

George McClellan was in charge of the Union Army at Antietam. After this fight he was relieved of command by President Lincoln, whom he would challenge as the Democratic candidate for president in the 1864 election.

"Lee's Army was ruined, and the end of the Confederacy was in sight,"[4] said a Confederate officer.

However, McClellan was unnerved by the slaughter that his troops had endured so far. He thought Lee was readying a huge mass of troops for a counter-attack, so he held off on putting any fresh troops into the gap. (In reality, Lee had no troops with which to stage a counterattack.)

Meanwhile, at another location, federal troops under General Ambrose E. Burnside were supposed to have crossed Antietam Creek early that morning and be attacking the Confederates they found. By doing so, they were supposed to keep Lee from shifting troops away from that area to other parts of the battle where the Confederates needed help.

Despite his difficulties at Antietam, Ambrose Burnside was promoted to replace McClellan when Lincoln relieved him. Unfortunately Burnside was no better a general, and led the Union Army to a disastrous defeat at Fredericksburg.

Antietam Creek was just 30 feet wide and shallow enough to be crossed in several places. However, Burnside focused on crossing the creek over a narrow stone bridge called the Rohrbach Bridge. Although it is estimated he had about 13,000 men to the Confederates' 4,000, Burnside kept sending small groups of Union soldiers to try to cross the bridge. They were easy targets for the Confederates waiting on the other side, and so the Northern troops kept getting driven back. The bridge has since been known as Burnside's Bridge.

Early in the afternoon, the Union troops finally got across the bridge and pushed the Confederates back. Within two hours, Burnside had most of his troops across the creek and was about to capture the only road that the Confederate Army could retreat on. If that happened, and there was no escape route, Lee knew that his army could be destroyed. As Lee anxiously watched the battle, he suddenly saw the flags of more troop regiments appear on a distant road and move toward him. If it was more Union soldiers, the Confederates were doomed. However, it was Confederate soldiers. Setting out from Harpers Ferry early that morning, they had marched 17 miles as fast as they could, and arrived at Antietam at just the right moment to save the Confederate army. They smashed into Burnside's troops, stopping them cold.

Finally, the single bloodiest day of battle during the Civil War was over. Or was it?

***

One day over a century later, the sun had set on Antietam Battlefield. Darkness crept across the ground, and eerie shadows formed.

A group of men were getting their last look at Burnside's Bridge and the woods surrounding it before it was time to leave. They crossed the old stone bridge one last time. The darkness was advancing over everything, like a big blanket, and they knew they had to leave shortly.

Suddenly one of the men pointed to the woods just beyond the bridge. A small ball of floating blue light, no bigger than a baseball, had appeared by one of the trees. As the men watched, the light began darting around from tree to tree.

As everyone wondered what the light was, another ball of blue light appeared . . . then another . . . and another. The woods were now filled with the blue orbs.

Mysterious blue orbs have been reported at the site of Burnside's Bridge on the Antietam Battlefield. Could these orbs be supernatural in nature?

They raced around, darting to and fro, moving faster and faster, zipping behind trees, skimming over the ground, soaring into the air.

And they were getting closer to the bridge.

All at once, the faint but unmistakable sound of a military drum could be heard. The drum was beating out a march—*rat-a-tat-tat, rat-a-tat-tat*—and as it did, the blue balls of light continued toward the bridge.

Burnside's Bridge is peaceful now, as compared to during the battle when it was a place of violence and death. Maybe, however, all of that killing has led to its being haunted.

That was the last thing the men heard or saw. Turning as one, they all ran to their car and jumped in. As the car pulled away from the darkness that now covered Burnside's Bridge, they saw the blue lights start to cross the bridge, just like the Union troops had done over 100 years before.

The men looked at each other. The hair on the backs of their necks rose. What had they just witnessed? Were those blue orbs the souls of the Union soldiers who had died trying to cross Burnside's Bridge? And what would have happened to the men if they had stayed on the bridge as the orbs swarmed all around?

Someone nervously laughed. No one wanted to find out the answer to that last question.

Few Civil War generals had as much of an up-and-down career as Ambrose E. Burnside, from whose name comes the word "sideburns" because of his distinctive facial hair.

Burnside was born on May 23, 1824, in Liberty, Indiana. He attended West Point in 1843 and graduated in 1847. After several years in the army, he resigned in 1853 to devote all his energy to a weapon he had invented known as the Burnside carbine. He had a large contract with the U.S. Army to produce the gun for them, but the army cancelled the contract and sent Burnside into a financial tailspin.

At the outbreak of the Civil War, he organized a volunteer regiment of Union troops that rushed to the defense of Washington, D.C. He then led a group of soldiers in a successful assault on the North Carolina coast. Burnside was ultimately given command of two corps of Union troops during the battle of Antietam, but his disjointed attempts to quickly take what became known as "Burnside's Bridge" hurt his reputation.

Still, when President Lincoln wanted to replace McClellan after the battle of Antietam, he turned to Burnside. Burnside had turned down the post before because he didn't think himself qualified. He reluctantly accepted the second time. At the Battle of Fredericksburg in December 1862, Burnside suffered a horrible defeat, losing 13,000 men. Shortly thereafter, he was reassigned.

Later in the war, Burnside had success in defending Knoxville, but followed with failure at the Battle of the Crater in Petersburg, Virginia. After this debacle, Burnside again resigned from the army. He died in 1881.

Ambrose Burnside

CHAPTER

FIVE

SUN GOING BACKWARDS

At length, we sought some stacks, and a barn, resolved not to ride farther; but there, on the straw and in the buildings, were the dead.[1]
—George W. Beale, Confederate Army

When night finally fell, and darkness ended the battle, the scenes of devastation and destruction were everywhere. The battlefield was covered with dead horses; blown-apart wooden wagons; smashed cannon; discarded muskets, rifles, and knives; and scattered canteens, bedrolls, and other pieces of equipment. Above all, there were the dead men, their eyes staring sightlessly at the night sky, their blood collecting in dark pools on the ground. The men who hadn't been killed, but were wounded, lay in all sorts of contorted positions, crying and sobbing and moaning and calling for water or assistance.

"No tongue can tell, no mind can conceive, no pen portray the horrible sights I witnessed," wrote one horror-stricken soldier.[2]

★ ★ ★ ★ ★ ★ ★ ★ ★ ★ ★ ★ ★ ★ ★ ★ ★ ★ ★

When the Antietam battle ended, the Sunken Road was filled with men who had been suddenly and violently killed.

For the soldiers it was the longest of days. "The sun seemed almost to go backwards, and it appeared as if night would never come," said one soldier.[3]

The next day it seemed likely that the battle would resume. The Union had received reinforcements during the night. McClellan had many fresh troops (they had not seen action the previous day), and so another opportunity presented itself for him to do serious damage to the Confederate Army.

However, as usual, McClellan was cautious, and convinced that Lee still had more men than he. So he did not attack. The next day the rebel army retreated to Virginia. McClellan did not initially pursue them, which angered many in his army, because they felt that the Confederates were weak and hurting and could have been defeated easily.

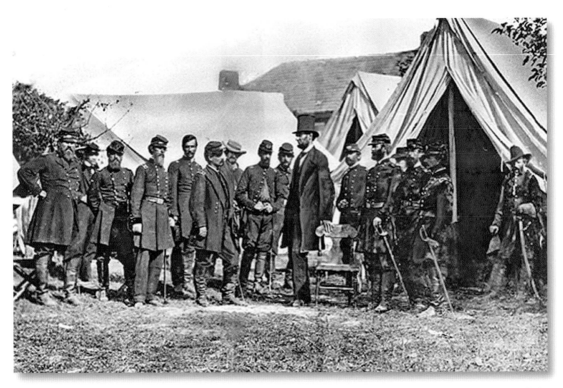

President Lincoln visited McClellan after Antietam. When the general didn't have his army pursue the retreating Confederates quickly enough for Lincoln, he was replaced as commander.

President Lincoln was also furious at McClellan for not going after the wounded Confederates. When the general showed no haste in subsequently chasing the rebel army, Lincoln replaced him in early November with Burnside. McClellan went home to New Jersey, where he spent the rest of the war.

Although Antietam was virtually a draw, it did stop the Confederate invasion. Lincoln could, and did, consider it a victory, which was just what he had been waiting for so he could issue the Emancipation Proclamation, which ended slavery in the South.

St. Paul's Church

The armies marched away from Antietam to continue the fight. The war would continue for almost three more years, until April 1865. However, some say the war still continues for some. . . .

***

In the middle of the town of Sharpsburg is the St. Paul Episcopal Church. As the battle raged, this church was used as a Confederate field hospital. Wounded and dying men were taken there, clothes soaked in blood and screaming in pain. They were attended to by overworked surgeons, who often had to amputate limbs to save lives.

Now, some say that on certain nights, if you listen hard enough, you can still hear the screams of soldiers as they endured the agonies of amputation or the pain of their wounds. Sometimes, it is said, strange lights can also be seen near the church's tower.

The Piper House was another place that rang with the agonized cries of the dead and dying. Some say these cries can still be heard there.

Are these the souls of men who were savagely and suddenly taken from this life?

On the battlefield is the Piper House. During the battle, it served as the headquarters for Confederate General James Longstreet, and its barn was a field hospital. Afterward, the bodies of three dead soldiers were removed from under the home's piano.

Now, just like at the church, it is said that the agonizing screams of the wounded and dying can be heard there. Others claim that mysterious figures suddenly appear in the house and then vanish without warning.

Is the Battle of Antietam still being fought here? Will it ever end, or are these poor souls doomed to fight until the end of time?

Besides hoping to stop the Confederate invasion of the North, President Lincoln had another reason for wanting a Union victory at Antietam: He wanted to issue the Emancipation Proclamation.

Lincoln wanted to strike at the Confederacy's advantage in having slaves to support its economy while its men went off to war. He also wanted to make the war about more than just restoring the federal union of states. He had to prevent Great Britain and France from potentially advancing on the United States. Finally, it was the right thing to do: Lincoln had always been against slavery.

On September 22, Lincoln issued the preliminary Emancipation Proclamation. It stated that Confederate states that had not returned to the Union by January 1, 1863, would have their slaves freed forever by that date.

Although Lincoln was ridiculed for freeing slaves in states that were not under Union control, with this document he completely changed the war. Now it was a war for freedom, not just a war to preserve the Union. Now no foreign country would come to the aid of the South, because to do so would be to support slavery.

Even though Antietam wasn't a great military victory, it did change the entire outcome of the war.

The first reading of the Emancipation Proclamation

During the four-year Civil War, over 10,000 military actions took place. There were 50 major battles, and more than 100 significantly affected the war. The events listed here involve the major players of the battle of Antietam.

1860   Abraham Lincoln is elected president.

1861   April 12   The Civil War begins with the Battle of Fort Sumter, South Carolina.

       July 21   In the First Battle of Bull Run, the Union Army suffers a surprising defeat.

       November 7   General Ulysses S. Grant begins his Civil War career at the Battle of Belmont in Missouri.

1862   March 8–9   The Battle of Hampton Roads off the coast of Virginia is the first battle between ironclad warships (the *Merrimack* and the *Monitor*).

       August 28–30   The Confederates defeat the Union at the Second Battle of Bull Run (Second Manassas).

       September 4   General Robert E. Lee crosses the Potomac River from Virginia into Maryland.

       September 13   Corporal Barton W. Mitchell finds Special Orders, No. 191.

       September 15   McClellan lines his troops for battle on the hills behind Antietam Creek.

       September 17   The Battle of Antietam begins at dawn.

       September 22   Lincoln issues the preliminary Emancipation Proclamation.

       November 3   Israel B. Richardson dies at the Pry House from wounds he sustained at Antietam.

       December 11–15   Ambrose Burnside leads the Union Army in a disastrous defeat at Fredericksburg.

1863   January 1   The Emancipation Proclamation takes effect.

       April 30–May 6   Union General Joseph Hooker is defeated at the Battle of Chancellorsville, Virginia.

       July 1–3   A Union victory at Gettysburg, the largest campaign of the Civil War, marks the end of Robert E. Lee's second invasion of the North.

1864   May 5–7   The Battle of the Wilderness in Spotsylvania County, Virginia, is the first clash between Robert E. Lee and Ulysses S. Grant.

1865   April 8   Lee surrenders his army to Ulysses S. Grant at Appomattox Courthouse, Virginia, effectively ending the Civil War. The next week, Lincoln is assassinated.

Chapter One

1. *Voices of the Civil War—Antietam.* The Editors of Time-Life Books. (Alexandria, VA: Time-Life Books, 1996), p. 17.

2. James McPherson, *Crossroads of Freedom: Antietam.* (New York: Oxford University Press, 2002), p. 107.

3. Ibid., p. 108.

4. Christopher K. Coleman, *Ghosts and Haunts of the Civil War.* (Nashville: Rutledge Hill Press, 1999), p. 54.

Chapter Two

1. *Voices of the Civil War—Antietam.* The Editors of Time-Life Books. (Alexandria, VA: Time-Life Books, 1996), p. 25.

2. James McPherson, *Crossroads of Freedom: Antietam.* (New York: Oxford University Press, 2002), p. 89.

3. Shelby Foote, *The Civil War: A Narrative.* Fort Sumter to Perryville. (New York: Vintage Books, 1958), p. 663.

4. Stephen W. Sears, *Landscape Turned Red.* (New York: Ticknor & Fields, 1983) p. 83.

5. Ibid, p. 85.

6. Ibid.

7. James McPherson, *Crossroads of Freedom: Antietam.* (New York: Oxford University Press, 2002), p. 86.

8. Ibid, p. 104.

Chapter Three

1. *Voices of the Civil War—Antietam.* The Editors of Time-Life Books. (Alexandria, VA: Time-Life Books, 1996), p. 60.

2. James McPherson, *Battle Cry of Freedom*. (New York: Oxford University Press, 1988), p. 537.

3. Stephen W. Sears, *Landscape Turned Red*. (New York: Ticknor & Fields, 1983) p. 167.

4. Ibid, p. 184.

5. Shelby Foote, *The Civil War: A Narrative*. Fort Sumter to Perryville. (New York: Vintage Books, 1958), p. 668.

6. James McPherson, *Crossroads of Freedom: Antietam*. (New York: Oxford University Press, 2002), p. 117.

7. Ibid, p. 118.

Chapter Four

1. *Voices of the Civil War—Antietam*. The Editors of Time-Life Books. (Alexandria, VA: Time-Life Books, 1996), p. 69.

2. Stephen W. Sears, *Landscape Turned Red*. (New York: Ticknor & Fields, 1983) p. 238.

3. Ibid, p. 240.

4. James McPherson, *Battle Cry of Freedom*. (New York: Oxford University Press, 1988), p. 543.

Chapter Five

1. *Voices of the Civil War—Antietam*. The Editors of Time-Life Books. (Alexandria, VA: Time-Life Books, 1996), p. 131.

2. James McPherson, *Crossroads of Freedom: Antietam*. (New York: Oxford University Press, 2002), p. 129.

3. Stephen W. Sears, *Landscape Turned Red*. (New York: Ticknor & Fields, 1983) p. 269.

FURTHER READING

Books

Dougherty, Terri. *America's Deadliest Day*. Mankato, MN: Capstone Press, 2008.

Nardo, Don. *Civil War Witness*. Mankato, MN: Compass Point Books, 2013.

Ratliff, Thomas. *You Wouldn't Want to Be a Civil War Soldier*. Danbury, CT: Children's Press, 2013.

Silvey, Anita. *I'll Pass for Your Comrade*. New York: Clarion Books, 2008.

Vansant, Wayne. *Grant vs. Lee*. Minneapolis: Zenith Press, 2013.

Works Consulted

Coleman, Christopher K. *Ghosts and Haunts of the Civil War*. Nashville: Rutledge Hill Press, 1999.

Foote, Shelby. *The Civil War: A Narrative*. Fort Sumter to   Perryville. New York: Vintage Books, 1958.

Gindlesperger, James and Suzanne. *So You Think You Know Antietam?* Winston-Salem, NC: John F. Blair, Publisher, 2012.

McPherson, James. *Battle Cry of Freedom*. New York: Oxford University Press, 1988.

McPherson, James. *Crossroads of Freedom: Antietam*. New York: Oxford University Press, 2002.

Reasoner, James. Antietam. *Nashville: Cumberland House,* 2000.

Roberts, Nancy. *Civil War Ghosts and Legends*. New York: Metro Books, 2002.

Sears, Stephen W. *Landscape Turned Red*. New York: Ticknor & Fields, 1983.

Varhola, Michael J. *Everyday Life During the Civil War*. Cincinnati: Writer's Digest Books, 1999.

Voices of the Civil War—Antietam. The Editors of Time-Life Books. Alexandria, VA: Time-Life Books, 1996.

FURTHER READING

On the Internet

American History for Kids: American Civil War

> http://www.historyforkids.org/learn/northamerica/after1500/history/civilwar.htm

The Civil War

> http://thecivil-war.com/civil-war-for-kids/

Ghosts of Antietam

> http://www.militaryghosts.com/antietam.html

Haunted Maryland: The Antietam National Battlefield

> http://www.prairieghosts.com/antietam.html

North versus South at Antietam Creek

Condemn (kuhn-DEM)—To judge harshly.

Contort—To twist or bend.

Eerie (EER-ee)—Weird.

Envelop (en-VELL-up)—To cover entirely.

Incompetent (in-KOM-pih-tint)—Lacking ability.

Intercept (in-ter-SEPT)—To interrupt the course of.

Legitimate (luh-JIT-uh-mit)—Lawful.

Linger—To stay in one place longer than expected.

Orb—Globe; sphere.

Peculiar (pih-KYOOL-yer)—Strange.

Preliminary (pre-LIH-muh-nayr-ee)—Leading up to the main part.

Prevail (pree-VAYL)—To win.

Renovate (REN-uh-vayt)—To restore to good condition.

Ridicule (RIH-duh-kyool)—To make fun of.

Tailspin—A collapse into failure.